Fairy Tale Creatures
Gnomes

by Mark L. Lewis

FOCUS READERS®

BEACON

www.focusreaders.com

Copyright © 2022 by Focus Readers®, Lake Elmo, MN 55042. All rights reserved. No part of this book may be reproduced or utilized in any form or by any means without written permission from the publisher.

Focus Readers is distributed by North Star Editions:
sales@northstareditions.com | 888-417-0195

Produced for Focus Readers by Red Line Editorial.

Photographs ©: Shutterstock Images, cover, 1, 4, 7, 8, 11, 12, 14, 17, 18, 20–21, 22, 24, 27, 29

Library of Congress Cataloging-in-Publication Data
Names: Lewis, Mark L., author.
Title: Gnomes : fairy tale creatures / by Mark L. Lewis.
Description: Lake Elmo, MN : Focus Readers, [2022] | Series: Fairy tale creatures | Includes index. | Audience: Grades 2-3
Identifiers: LCCN 2021006321 (print) | LCCN 2021006322 (ebook) | ISBN 9781637390047 (hardcover) | ISBN 9781637390115 (paperback) | ISBN 9781637390184 (ebook) | ISBN 9781637390245 (pdf)
Subjects: LCSH: Gnomes--Juvenile literature.
Classification: LCC GR549 .L49 2022 (print) | LCC GR549 (ebook) | DDC 398.21--dc23
LC record available at https://lccn.loc.gov/2021006321
LC ebook record available at https://lccn.loc.gov/2021006322

Printed in the United States of America
Mankato, MN
082021

About the Author

Mark L. Lewis writes books for young readers in his spare time. He works on a farm and wishes he had gnomes to help him.

Table of Contents

CHAPTER 1
Master Gardeners 5

CHAPTER 2
Gnomes of the World 9

CHAPTER 3
Short and Round 15

Garden Gnomes 20

CHAPTER 4
Living Together 23

Focus on Gnomes • 28
Glossary • 30
To Learn More • 31
Index • 32

Chapter 1

Master Gardeners

A full moon shone on the garden. A group of gnomes walked through the bushes. Their tools clanked. The gnomes came out each night to take care of the plants.

 Gnomes use magic to help flowers stay healthy and beautiful.

The gnomes yanked weeds from the dirt. They checked each flower. A few flowers had wilted. Their leaves drooped.

The gnomes touched the stems. Magic flowed through their fingertips. Each plant's leaves became greener. The petals perked up, too.

Fun Fact

In some stories, gnomes are statues that come to life at night.

 Gnomes can use tools such as watering cans and shovels to care for plants.

The gnomes worked hard to keep the garden clean. They trimmed branches. They picked up sticks from the grass.

Soon, dawn approached. The gnomes ducked back into the dirt. They did not want anyone to know that they had been working.

Chapter 2

Gnomes of the World

Many people **associate** gnomes with gardens. But that is not how stories of gnomes first started. Early **legends** said gnomes were miners. They worked underground.

 The kind of work that gnomes do has changed over time.

People believed gnomes led human miners through tunnels. The gnomes showed the miners where to dig.

Many of these early stories came from the Netherlands and Germany. The stories may have been **inspired** by tales of other beings. Those include dwarfs, fairies, and trolls.

Fun Fact

People in **ancient** Rome put gnome-like statues in their gardens for protection.

 Some gnomes that live in forests can talk to animals.

Gnomes share some traits with them. For example, all tend to be small. And they can often do magic.

Over time, people moved to new places. They brought their legends.

 In some stories, gnomes make their homes out of mushrooms.

The stories changed as they spread. Most legends still said gnomes lived underground. But the gnomes were no longer miners. Instead, they took care of the earth. They helped trees and gardens grow.

Meanwhile, other **cultures** told their own stories of gnome-like creatures. These creatures often lived in forests or under the ground. In some stories, they were builders. Others were said to help people on farms. They cared for plants and animals.

Hawaiian stories tell of gnomes called eepa. The eepa built a temple in the forest for the gods.

Chapter 3

Short and Round

In many stories, gnomes are short and round. They are often less than 2 feet (0.6 m) tall. Some are a bit taller. But gnomes are never as tall as humans.

Some gnomes are just a few inches tall.

Over time, some **descriptions** of gnomes changed. Many older stories only talked about male gnomes. These gnomes had hunched backs. Their skin was wrinkled. They also had long, white beards.

Later stories describe both male and female gnomes. These gnomes often have big heads and small bodies. Many have large noses, too. One story says gnomes look like potatoes with legs.

 Young gnomes appear more often in newer art and stories.

In newer stories, gnomes wear clothes with bright colors. Blue, red, and green are the most common. Gnomes tend to wear pointed hats as well.

 Scandinavian gnomes tend to have long, white beards.

In some stories, gnomes are quiet and shy. They try to avoid people. For example, one story tells of small men that hide in trees. When a person sees the small men, they stop time and disappear.

Other gnomes are friendly and fun. In **Scandinavia**, gnomes are associated with Christmas. They are said to bring people presents. These gnomes can make friends with people. But they can also play tricks.

In Scandinavia, a gnome is sometimes called a *tomte*, *nisse*, or *tonttu*.

STORY SPOTLIGHT

Garden Gnomes

Gnomes have been linked to gardens for many years. People began making statues of gnomes in the 1800s. At first, the statues were meant to stay inside. But soon, people began to set them outside near flowers. People still place statues of gnomes in their gardens today.

The largest collection of garden gnomes is at the Gnome Reserve. This garden is in England. It has more than 2,000 garden gnomes. Its owners say the gnomes take care of the garden. People come to see the gnomes. They also admire the beautiful flowers and plants.

Garden gnomes became popular decorations in Europe in the 1840s.

Chapter 4

Living Together

Most stories say gnomes live in groups. In one story, gnomes have a king. His name is Gob. He leads the gnomes. They live together in huge palaces made of stone. These palaces are underground.

Gnomes often live in places with hills or trees.

 Some gnomes make small homes in tree trunks. Others dig burrows.

Groups of gnomes sometimes live together in places called Gnome Eggs. These round **structures** sit

24

above the ground. A Gnome Egg is invisible to most people. But inside, it looks like a castle. Tunnels lead to many rooms and halls.

Gnome Eggs help gnomes stay hidden. They are up on mountains or deep in the woods. Even so, people sometimes find Gnome Eggs. Some people even go inside.

Some stories say the gnome king has a magical sword.

They visit the magical world where gnomes live.

Other gnomes live near homes or farms. They help the people who live there. But people must be careful. If they don't take good care of their homes or animals, gnomes could punish them. In Scandinavia,

Fun Fact

Legends say setting out a bowl of porridge for gnomes could make them happy.

 In Sweden, some families set out rice pudding for gnomes on Christmas Eve.

gnomes are said to love **tradition**. They get mad if people make too many changes.

All stories of gnomes are a little different. Each story is shaped by the people telling it. And people continue to tell new stories.

27

FOCUS ON
Gnomes

Write your answers on a separate piece of paper.

1. Write two to three sentences describing the main ideas of Chapter 4.

2. What other stories have changed over time? Why do you think those stories changed?

3. In early stories, what job did most gnomes do?
    - **A.** They were gardeners.
    - **B.** They were miners.
    - **C.** They were kings.

4. How would being located on mountains or in forests help Gnome Eggs stay hidden?
    - **A.** These places are easy to walk to.
    - **B.** These places are near many animals.
    - **C.** These places are far from where most people live.

5. What does **drooped** mean in this book?

*A few flowers had wilted. Their leaves **drooped**.*

    A. sagged or hung down
    B. filled with water
    C. glowed in the dark

6. What does **admire** mean in this book?

*People come to see the gnomes. They also **admire** the beautiful flowers and plants.*

    A. to run from
    B. to throw away
    C. to look at and enjoy

Answer key on page 32.

Glossary

ancient
Very old or from long ago.

associate
To connect one thing with something else.

cultures
Groups of people and the ways they live, including their customs, beliefs, and laws.

descriptions
Ways of telling what a thing is, does, or looks like.

inspired
Based on or shaped by something or someone else.

legends
Well-known stories from the past. Some legends are based on facts, but not all legends are true.

Scandinavia
An area in northern Europe that includes the countries of Norway, Sweden, and Denmark. Finland and Iceland may also be included.

structures
Things, such as buildings, that are built by joining together smaller parts.

tradition
A way of doing something that is passed down over many years.

To Learn More

BOOKS

Gagliardi, Sue. *Fairies*. Lake Elmo, MN: Focus Readers, 2019.

Krensky, Stephen. *The Book of Mythical Beasts & Magical Creatures*. New York: DK Publishing, 2020.

London, Martha. *Gnomes*. Minneapolis: Abdo Publishing, 2020.

NOTE TO EDUCATORS

Visit **www.focusreaders.com** to find lesson plans, activities, links, and other resources related to this title.

Index

A
animals, 13, 26

G
gardens, 5, 7, 9–10, 12, 20
Germany, 10
Gnome Eggs, 24–25
Gob, 23

H
hats, 17

M
magic, 6, 11, 25–26
miners, 9–10, 12

N
Netherlands, 10

P
plants, 5–6, 13, 20

S
Scandinavia, 19, 26

T
tricks, 19
tunnels, 10, 25

Answer Key: **1.** Answers will vary; **2.** Answers will vary; **3.** B; **4.** C; **5.** A; **6.** C